Colonial People

≈ The ≈
Woodworkers

Bobbie Kalman & Deanna Brady

Illustrations by Bonna Rouse

 Crabtree Publishing
www.crabtreebooks.com

Created by Bobbie Kalman

Dedicated by Bonna Rouse
To my niece Zoie Irwin,
born during the production of this book

Editor-in-Chief
Bobbie Kalman

Writing team
Bobbie Kalman
Deanna Brady
Kathryn Smithyman

Project editor
Kathryn Smithyman

Editors
Niki Walker
Amanda Bishop

Computer design
Margaret Amy Reiach
Robert MacGregor (cover)

Production coordinator
Heather Fitzpatrick

Photo researchers
Heather Fitzpatrick
Jaimie Nathan

Consultant
Prof. Mario Rodriguez, Dept. of Restoration
Fashion Institute of Technology, NY

Special thanks to
Old Salem, Peter Crabtree, Marc Crabtree

Photographs
Colonial Williamsburg Foundation: title page,
pages 7, 14, 16, 22, 23 (bottom), 24, 26-27, 30
Photos courtesy of Old Salem, Winston-Salem,
N.C.: pages 5, 19, 20
Bobbie Kalman: page 23 (top)

Illustrations
All illustrations by Bonna Rouse except
the following:
Barbara Bedell: pages 6, 13 (top right),
14 (bottom right), 15, 17 (bottom),
19 (bottom left), 24, 26, 30
Margaret Amy Reiach: page 16
Lewis Parker: page 28

Digital prepress
Embassy Graphics

Printer
Worzalla Publishing Company

Crabtree Publishing Company

www.crabtreebooks.com   1-800-387-7650

PMB 16A	612 Welland Ave.	73 Lime Walk
350 Fifth Ave.,	St. Catharines,	Headington
Suite 3308	Ontario,	Oxford
New York, NY	Canada	OX3 7AD
10118	L2M 5V6	United Kingdom

Cataloging-in-Publication Data
Kalman, Bobbie
  The woodworkers / Bobbie Kalman and Deanna Brady;
illustrated by Bonna Rouse.
    p. cm. -- (Colonial people)
  Includes index.
  Discusses the importance of wood in colonial times, describing how trees
were cut down and made into lumber and the training of apprentice
carpenters, cabinetmakers, coopers, and wheelwrights.
    ISBN 0-7787-0744-X (RLB) -- ISBN 0-7787-0790-3 (pbk.)
    1. Woodwork--United States--History--Juvenile literature.
  2. Woodworkers--United States--History--Juvenile literature. 3. United
States--Social life and customs--To 1775--Juvenile literature. [1. Woodwork.
  2. United States--Social life and customs--To 1775.] I. Bedell, Barbara, ill.
II. Title. III. Series: Kalman, Bobbie. Colonial people.
  TT180 .K35 2002
  684'.08'0974--dc21
                                                    2001047525

Contents

Making things from wood

In **colonial** times, forests covered most of North America. **Colonists**, or the people who lived in the **colonies**, crafted all kinds of objects from wood. They made fences, wagons, wheels, ships, **barrels**, trunks, furniture, dishes, and paper from the trees that grew nearby.

Most people had the skills to make basic wooden items for their homes and farms. When a farmer needed a container in which to carry food for his oxen, he carved one from a log. Many men spent their evenings carving simple furniture and handles for their tools. They shaped wooden toys from small pieces of wood by **whittling**, or shaving off chips with a knife.

Early homes

Colonists also built wooden houses. Most men knew how to cut down trees and build simple log homes for their families. They built the walls of the homes by stacking logs one on top of the other. Most early colonial homes were log homes.

Later homes

Although families often built their first homes, people began building larger homes as towns grew. These larger houses, called **frame houses**, were constructed using a frame of squared logs (see page 9). Many people hired woodworkers to build frame houses because building them required greater skill. Woodworkers also built shops, churches, and other buildings in town.

Notches were cut into the logs so they would fit snugly and stay in place. The spaces between the logs were filled in with grass or straw and mud.

This photograph shows two styles of colonial homes. The house in the foreground was built by stacking squared logs. The house in the background is a frame house.

Who were the woodworkers?

Wood became an important source of jobs and income in the colonies. As towns grew, skilled woodworkers started **specializing**, or becoming experts at certain jobs. There was so much work that a specialized woodworker could earn a living doing just one type of job, or **trade**.

The woodworking trades

Tradesmen who built houses were called **housewrights**. **Coopers** made barrels and other containers, **cabinetmakers** made furniture, **wheelwrights** made wheels, **wainwrights** made carriages, and **shipwrights** built ships. Each of these specialized woodworkers worked in colonial towns. Read on to discover more about each of these trades.

Who made what?

Look at the photograph on page 7 and find five things made from wood. Name three woodworkers who worked on the houses. Who made the furniture inside the houses? What was the tradesman who made barrels called? Do not worry if you do not know the answers yet. You will by the time you have finished reading this book!

Several housewrights worked together to complete large frame houses, such as the one shown right.

7

Skilled woodsmen

Woodsmen cut down trees and prepared the wood for other woodworkers to use. Woodsmen were also called **axmen** because they used a **felling ax** to cut down trees. Skilled woodsmen looked for healthy trees with straight trunks because they knew that these trees produced the best **lumber**. Woodworkers used lumber to construct homes and other buildings.

"Timber!"

Cutting down trees was dangerous work. A falling tree moved so fast that sometimes a person could not get out of its way. A tree could easily crush someone under its weight! Woodsmen had to be very careful when they **felled**, or cut down, trees. Before they made any cuts, they checked the direction of the wind. Even a slight breeze could change the direction in which a tree fell.

An axman, shown left, made the first notch, or cut, near the bottom of a tree's trunk. He cut another notch opposite the first one. The axman chopped at the second notch to cut away more of the tree. When enough wood was cut from the trunk, the upper part of the tree started to tilt toward the first notch. Soon, the whole tree fell. Some woodsmen could fell a tree with as few as eight cuts!

Trimming and bucking

Once the **timber**, or felled tree, was on the ground, the woodsman trimmed off the branches with a **broad ax.** Unless very long pieces of wood were needed, he **bucked** the tree, or cut it into shorter logs. To buck the tree, he stood on top of the trunk and chopped deep notches into either side. He then cut through the timber where the two notches met in the middle. The woodsman kept making cuts along the trunk until he had cut it into many short logs. Short logs were much easier to stack or move than longer logs.

barking irons

Peeling the bark

Most woodsmen peeled the bark off the trees they felled. Timber dried faster after the bark was removed. Woodsmen used wedge-shaped iron tools called **barking irons** or **peeling irons** to peel the bark. They pushed the irons along the log to shave off the bark in strips. The bark of a freshly cut tree came off easily.

Squaring the timber

Woodsmen sometimes squared the timber so it was easier to stack or transport. To square a log, they used a broad ax. First, they marked four lines along the the log to form a square and used the lines as guides to **hew**, or slice away, the rounded part of the log. A woodsman stood next to the log and hewed downward along one line, and then he cut along the line on the opposite side. He rolled the log onto one of the flat sides so it would not move while he cut the last two sides.

A broad ax had a wide blade that sliced all the way through a log.

From timber to lumber

Timber was stacked in piles and left to dry for at least one summer. The wood shrank as it dried. Wood that was dried in this way was called **seasoned** wood. It was used for building because it was hard and strong. If wood was not seasoned before it was used, it would shrink after a building was finished. Shrunken boards could make floors uneven or leave gaps in the walls.

Objects that needed to be sturdy were made from wood that was seasoned for a long time. Wood used to make wagon wheels, for example, was seasoned for at least four years. **Sawyers** sawed the seasoned logs into **planks** of lumber. They cut lumber for wainwrights, shipwrights, and housewrights. They measured and cut planks to the exact size builders needed for each project.

Marking wood

Sawyers cut logs into straight planks by following marks made with a **chalk line**. A chalk line was a long string coated with chalk, charcoal, or powdered **red ocher**. The sawyers stretched the chalk line along the top of a log and held it down at both ends. One sawyer pulled up the middle of the string and then released it. As the string snapped down against the log, the chalk was knocked off it and onto the wood, leaving a line.

The sawyers made chalk lines a few inches apart and then cut along them to make several long planks.

Types of saws

Sawyers used several types of saws. Saws had sharp teeth along their blades. Sawyers used a **cross-cut saw** (left) to cut a log to the length they needed. These long saws had two handles. A pair of sawyers worked together, pulling the saw back and forth across the log.

Working in a saw pit

When cutting boards or planks, sawyers sliced down the length of a log using a **pit saw**. The pit saw was a two-person saw. It was called a pit saw because the logs were placed over a **saw pit**, or deep trench dug into the ground. One sawyer stood on top of the log. His partner, called the **pit man** or **box man**, stood below it in the pit. The two men took turns pushing and pulling the long saw blade up and down to cut through the log.

The pit man had a dusty job! He often wore a broad-brimmed hat to shield his head and face from the falling sawdust.

The building trades

Carpenters made and repaired items from wood. During colonial times, they also constructed buildings. Carpenters who built homes were called housewrights. Housewrights built the **foundations**, or bases of buildings, and put together the frames for the walls and roofs. Some wealthy colonists hired expert carpenters, known as **master** builders, to design large houses.

Master builders supervised the **masons** as well as the woodworkers. Masons laid bricks for chimneys, fireplaces, and walls. **Joiners** were the carpenters who finished the woodwork on buildings. They "joined" together pieces of wood to make door and window frames, wall paneling, and flooring. Joiners also made plain chests, desks, tables, and chairs.

Tools of the trade

Housewrights and carpenters had a variety of tools. Most of their tools had wooden handles with iron parts that cut, shaved, drilled, smoothed, or carved wood. Each tool was well designed to do a specific job. A carpenter's tools were his prized possessions. He took great care to keep them clean and sharp.

Find the right tool!

Look at the picture on the left to see how these builders are using their tools. Match the tools mentioned below to the builders in the picture who are using them.

1. A carpenter is smoothing a **beam** with an **adze**. Which man is using an adze?

2. Which carpenter is using a **plane** to shave off the rough top layer of a plank?

3. A **boring auger** or **screw auger** made holes in wood. Which carpenter is using one?

4. A **mortise** hole (see top right diagram) was made by hammering a **mortise ax** with a **mallet**. Find the carpenter making a mortise.

5. Which carpenter is using a **ripsaw** to cut a wide plank into narrower planks?

6. Find the builder who is using a **froe** to split off **clapboards** that will cover the sides of the new house.

Types of joints

A **joint** is a place where two pieces of wood come together. Carpenters carefully carved joints so the pieces would fit snugly. They used different joints for different projects.

Mortise-and-tenon joints connected the beams in a house frame. Wooden pegs called **trunnels**, *or "tree nails," secured the joints.*

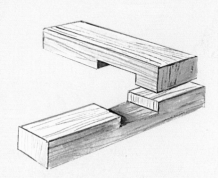

*A notch was cut into each piece of a **lap joint**. The notches were the same size, so the two pieces fit together snugly.*

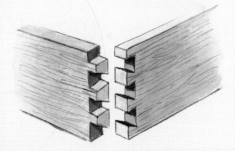

*The pieces of a **dovetail joint** had triangular parts, which fit so securely that they did not need nails to hold them together. Dovetail joints were used to make furniture parts such as drawers.*

Building a home

To begin building a house, workers dug trenches in the ground where the walls would stand. They lined the trenches with a thick layer of stones that kept water away from the base of the house. The stones had to be **level**, or even, so that the walls built over them would be straight. Next, workers laid heavy wooden beams, called **sills**, in the trenches. The sills formed the foundation on which the outside walls would stand. Carpenters made sure that the sills were perfectly level and that the corners were exactly square. If they were not, the walls built on them would not be straight or have square corners.

As carpenters finished the foundation, other workers dug out the ground underneath it to make a cellar. The cellar was used to store vegetables so they would not freeze or spoil.

The cellar entrance was located outside the house.

14

Making the wall frames

Carpenters built homes that would last. They constructed each wall using a heavy wooden frame called a **bent**. They laid out the wooden beams that were needed for each bent and put them together on the ground. They carved joints on each pair of beams by hand so they would fit only with one another. The carpenters then numbered each beam to keep track of where it should go. They joined the beams to form the bents, and when all four bents were ready, they positioned them on the sills. A group of men worked together to raise the heavy bents to form the frame of the house.

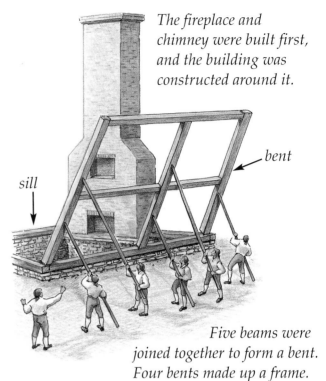

The fireplace and chimney were built first, and the building was constructed around it.

bent

sill

Five beams were joined together to form a bent. Four bents made up a frame.

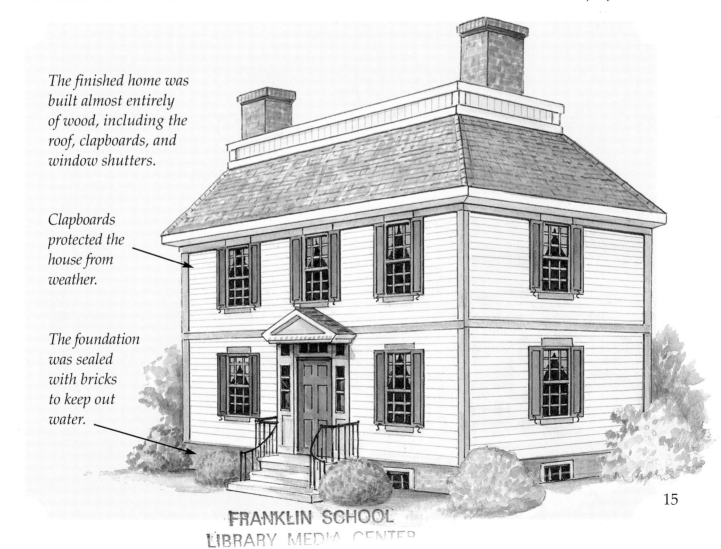

The finished home was built almost entirely of wood, including the roof, clapboards, and window shutters.

Clapboards protected the house from weather.

The foundation was sealed with bricks to keep out water.

Raising the roof

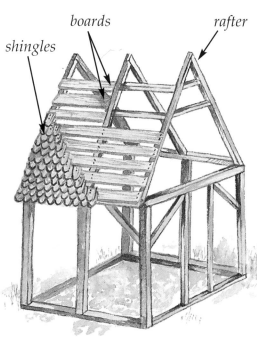

shingles   *boards*   *rafter*

Spaces were left between the boards to allow the wood to expand in hot weather without damaging the roof. Carpenters overlapped the shingles so that snow and rain would run off them.

After the carpenters completed the walls, they measured and cut long wooden roof beams called **rafters**. While the rafters were still on the ground, the carpenters carved joints into them and tested the joints to make sure they were snug. They then carried each rafter to the roof and put it in place.

Shingled roofs

The carpenters nailed long, flat boards across the rafters to secure them. They then covered the boards with **shingles**. Shingles were small, flat pieces of wood that fit together side by side. The carpenters nailed the shingles to the boards in rows. They worked up from the bottom of the roof, so that each row of shingles overlapped the top of the row below it. Shingled roofs kept rain from leaking into a house.

16

Making shingles

As demand for shingles grew, some woodworkers specialized in making only shingles. They became known as **shinglemakers**. Shingles were made from woods that did not rot easily, such as cypress or cedar. Using a froe, the shinglemaker split large pieces of wood into smaller sections. These small sections were known as **rough shingles**. Some people used rough shingles on their roofs, but shinglemakers also made shingles of a better quality. The better shingles were shaved smooth and provided more protection from wet weather than rough shingles did. They were **tapered**, or cut thinner on one end, so they would fit together snugly.

The shaving horse

The shinglemaker used a workbench called a **shaving horse**. He clamped a rough shingle to the horse and then sat at one end. He used a **drawknife** to trim and smooth the shingle a bit at a time until it was flat. The drawknife was named after the way it was used. It was **drawn**, or pulled, over wood. Carpenters, cabinetmakers, and coopers also sat at shaving horses and used drawknives to smooth wood.

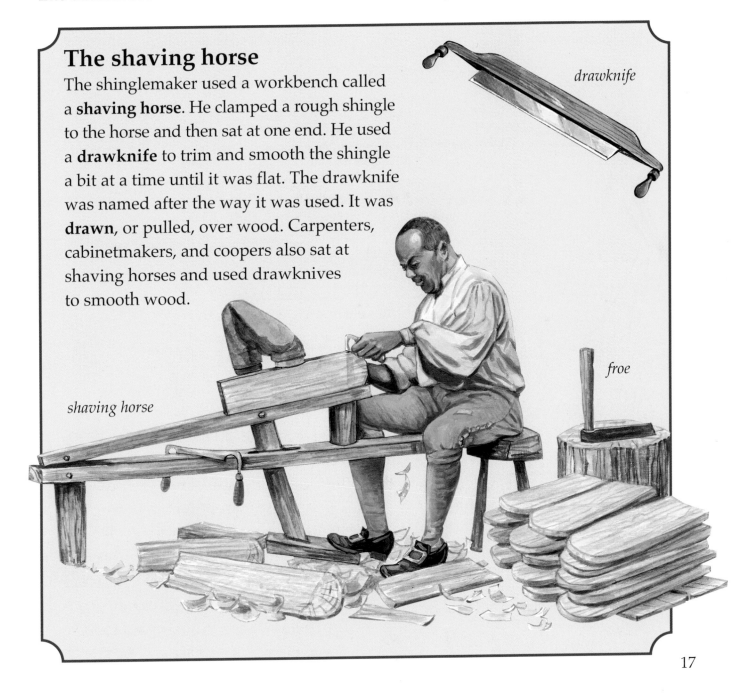

drawknife

froe

shaving horse

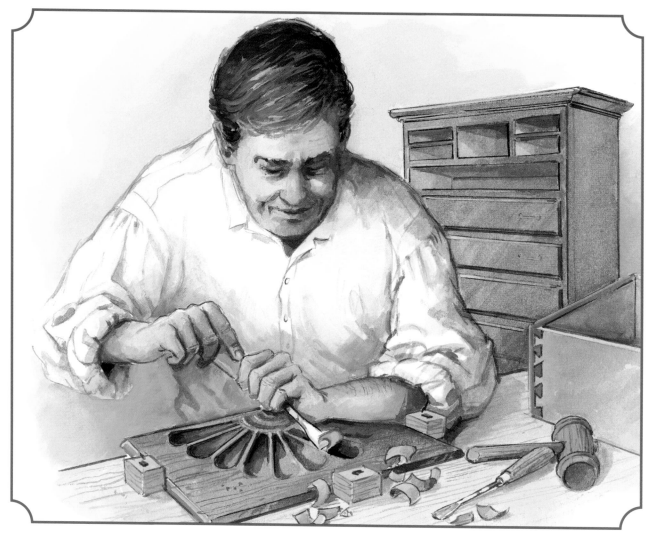

The cabinetmaker

Cabinetmakers were woodworkers who made fine furniture. Early cabinetmakers copied popular English styles of furniture to sell to the colonists. Over time, they began to design and produce their own styles of furniture as well. Many of the pieces were richly carved and decorated. Each craftsman added his own personal touches. Well known cabinetmakers often signed the furniture they made.

Cabinetmakers took pride in crafting quality work. They used special tools and selected the ideal type of wood for each piece of furniture. Oak, maple, pine, and cherry wood were used to make many kinds of furniture, but black walnut was the prized wood.

*The cabinetmaker above uses a **gouge** to carve decorative grooves into a piece of wood that will be part of the chest of drawers shown on page 19.*

Good looks for less

Some cabinetmakers made furniture from less expensive wood and covered it with **veneer.** Veneer was a thin sheet of fine wood that was glued to the surface of furniture. It gave a lower-priced piece of furniture an expensive appearance.

Finishing fine furniture

Before selling a piece of furniture, the cabinetmaker applied a **finish** to its outside surfaces. Finishes protected wood. They included stains, **varnishes**, vegetable dyes, and oils. The cabinetmaker rubbed the finish into the wood and polished it until it looked glossy and rich.

The cabinetmaker, shown right, made fine furniture, including chests of drawers (top right) and vanities (above). He also made coffins.

The cabinetmaker's shop

A cabinetmaker's shop was filled with woodworking tools. He used some tools to cut the pieces he needed to make tables, chairs, dressers, and other furniture. He used other tools to drill holes and carve designs into furniture. The cabinetmaker below is drilling a hole using a **bit** that is held in a **brace**.

The cabinetmaker's biggest and most important tool, however, was the **lathe**. He used it to shape rectangular pieces of wood into round poles. With a lathe, the cabinetmaker made **spindles** for staircases and legs for chairs, tables, and cabinets.

brace

bit

The cabinetmaker drills a hole by turning the brace in a circular motion.

To make a spindle, the cabinetmaker clamped a piece of wood into the lathe. His assistant turned the wheel while the cabinetmaker carved the spinning wood.

Working the lathe

The lathe was connected to a wheel that was turned by a hand crank, foot pedals, or running water. The wheel made the lathe spin. The larger the wheel, the faster it spun the lathe. The biggest wheel was called a **great wheel**.

A cabinetmaker who shaped wood on a lathe was called a **turner**. As the wood spun on the lathe, the turner carved and smoothed it. Every few minutes, his assistant stopped turning the wheel so the turner could measure the wood with his **calipers**, shown right.

The cooper

Coopers made **casks**, or wooden containers. There were many types of casks, and each one had a specific size, shape, and name. For example, **hogsheads** were large casks that were used to store and ship tobacco. Other casks included firkins, kilderkins, piggins, and rundlets, but barrels were the most common casks. Their curved sides made them ideal for moving goods from place to place. A barrel too heavy to lift was simply turned on its side and rolled. Coopers made casks out of thin wooden planks called **staves**. They cut the staves themselves and held them together with hoops. In the early years, hoops were made of wood. In later times, blacksmiths made iron hoops for barrels.

The cooper uses a curved drawknife to shape and smooth the inside of a stave.

Types of coopers

Some coopers specialized in making certain types of casks. **Dry** or **slack coopers** made casks for storing dry goods such as grain, flour, tobacco, and nails. **White coopers** made buckets, pails, butter churns, tubs, and vats used for dairy products such as milk and butter. Some farmers were able to make these casks themselves because these straight-sided containers were easier to make than barrels. **Tight coopers** had the greatest skill. They made watertight barrels and kegs that held liquids such as water, oil, molasses, beer, and wine. The sturdy containers they made sealed perfectly and did not leak. They were ideal for long sea voyages.

*The containers shown here are a barrel, a bucket, and a **churn**. Which was used to make butter? You were right if you said churn!*

Assembling a barrel

To make a barrel, a cooper stood a number of staves on end in a circle. He held the bottoms together with a strap called a **truss hoop**. He then heated the staves to make them flexible and tightened a rope around their tops to pull them together. As the tops of the staves moved inward, the middles curved out. The cooper then slid a hoop over the top of the newly formed barrel. He added more hoops to strengthen it and trimmed the ends of the staves so they were even. He fitted and hammered **heads**, or lids, into both ends of the barrel. Finally, the cooper drilled two holes into the barrel—one at the top and one on the side. Liquids were poured through the top hole, and people peeked through the side hole to check the contents of the barrel. Plugs sealed the holes.

The wheelwright

In most towns and cities, craftsmen called wheelwrights built wheels for wagons, carriages, carts, and wheelbarrows. To make a wheel, the wheelwright first crafted the **hub**, or center, of the wheel from a piece of wood that had been seasoned for several years.

The hub needed to be very strong because it held the wheel's spokes. The wheelwright fitted a hollow metal tube called a **box** into the center of the hub. The box held a rod called an **axle**, which connected a pair of wheels so they would roll together.

Fitting the spokes

After making the hub, the wheelwright carved a dozen or more wooden **spokes**. He cut square mortise holes around the outside of the hub and carved a tenon into the end of each spoke. He shaped each tenon to fit a mortise perfectly. He then tapped each spoke into its mortise with a sledgehammer. When all the spokes were in place, he hammered them tightly into the hub.

Making the rim

Once the spokes were attached to the hub, the wheelwright made the **rim** of the wheel. The rim was made up of six to eight curved sections of wood called **felloes**. The wheelwright cut two mortises into each felloe to hold two spokes. The tenon on the end of each spoke fit tightly into a mortise on the felloe.

Fitting the tire

A strip of iron called a **tire** went around the rim to tighten it and protect it from wear. The local blacksmith made the tires and often fitted them onto the wheels. The iron tire was heated to make it stretch and was slipped over the rim. The tire was then doused with water to cool it and make it shrink. As the tire shrank, it squeezed the felloes tightly together to make the wheel stronger.

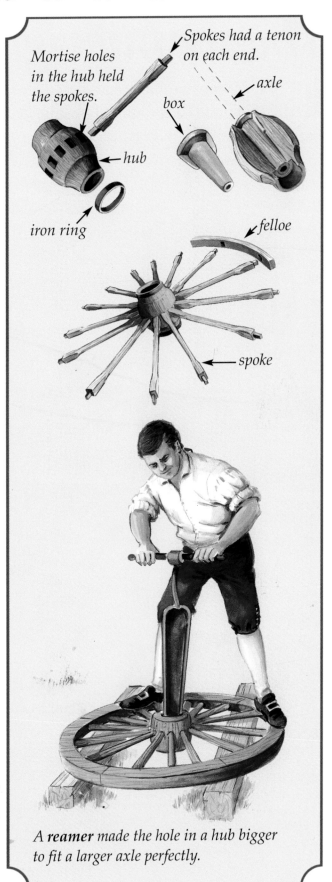

Mortise holes in the hub held the spokes.

Spokes had a tenon on each end.

axle

box

hub

iron ring

felloe

spoke

*A **reamer** made the hole in a hub bigger to fit a larger axle perfectly.*

25

The wainwright

To travel on land, many colonists rode horses or drove simple carts and wagons pulled by animals. Farmers often built their own carts and attached them to wheels made by a wheelwright. Some wheelwrights and joiners made and sold sturdy wagons and simple coaches, but as the colonists grew wealthier they wanted fancier transportation.

Woodworkers called wainwrights began making fine wagons, coaches, and carriages. A master wainwright employed several craftsmen, including wheelwrights, blacksmiths, and painters to make the carriages.

Cabinetmakers designed and carved the carriages, and upholsterers covered the seats with fabric.

The shipwright

Ships carried goods, lumber, tobacco, and people to Europe and brought back items that the colonists could not produce themselves. Shipwrights were woodworkers who designed and built ships. There was plenty of work for these craftsmen in every port.

So many trees grew in the colonies that wood was inexpensive. Colonists built ships at a lower cost than shipbuilders in Europe could build them. In time, most English merchants ordered their ships from colonial shipwrights, and shipbuilding became a big industry.

Building a ship

The first step in shipbuilding was crafting the **keel**, which ran along the bottom of the ship. It was like the ship's spine, to which shipwrights added "ribs." The ribs were the framework for the **hull**, or body, of the ship. To finish the hull, the shipwrights covered the ribs with planks. Once the planks were in place, a **caulker** filled in the gaps between them to seal the hull against leaks. He used tar and **oakum**, which was a stringy fiber that came from oak trees.

A **mastmaker** made the **masts**, which held up the sails. He carved them from tree trunks. The sails trapped the wind, which powered the ships. Sails were made of strong cloth in the shapes of rectangles or triangles.

Apprentice to journeyman

In the colonies, most children did not go to school. Many learned practical housekeeping and farming skills from their families, but some children trained to become tradespeople. To learn a trade, a child became an apprentice, or assistant, to a master craftsman.

Most apprentices were boys, but some girls were apprenticed to **milliners** or wigmakers. Apprentices were between ten and fifteen years old when they began studying a trade, which was usually chosen by their fathers. While they learned the skills of the trade, apprentices worked and studied without pay in the shops of their master's.

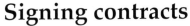

Signing contracts

A woodworking apprentice lived and studied with a master tradesman for four to seven years. Both the apprentice and the master signed a contract called an **indenture**. An indenture stated that the apprentice would receive food, clothing, shelter, and training. In return, the young man promised to obey the master and work hard for him as his assistant.

Learning on the job

At first, the apprentice did chores and ran errands to earn his keep. Over time, the master taught his apprentice the skills of the craft. An apprentice who worked in a cabinetmaker's shop learned how to turn a lathe and apply finishes to wood. A cooper's apprentice cut staves and kept the shop clean.

Making a masterpiece

When the apprentice had learned his craft well, he had to create a finished piece of work that would show his abilities. This test of his skill was judged by the master craftsman and was known as a "masterpiece." If the master decided the work was good enough, he released the apprentice from his indenture.

(opposite page) A young apprentice is learning how to design furniture under the supervision of a master craftsman.

Becoming a journeyman

After a young man finished his apprenticeship, he became a **journeyman**. A journeyman began earning a wage for his work in a busy workshop or on a building site. He could work for other tradespeople, open his own shop, or continue to work for his master for a wage.

Glossary

barrel A large container with round sides made of strips of wood joined together with hoops

beam A squared log used to form a house frame

broad ax A large ax with a wide blade

cabinetmaker A carpenter who made fine furniture by hand

calipers A tool made up of two arms that spread to measure the thickness of an object

carpenter A person who works with wood; in colonial times, a person who built houses

colonial Relating to living in a colony or to a period when European countries ruled North America

colonist A person who lives in a colony

colony An area ruled by a faraway country

cooper A person who made round wooden containers such as barrels and kegs

felling ax An ax used to chop down trees

foundation The base on which a house was built

frame The "skeleton" of walls and buildings made by fitting beams together

housewright A carpenter who built houses

joiner A person who cut and shaped pieces of wood to fit snugly together

joint The place where two pieces of wood are joined together

lumber Logs that are cut and ready for use in building and furniture making

master Describing an experienced or expert tradesperson

milliner A person who sold fashionable goods to colonists

notch A v-shaped cut in wood

plank A thick, flat wooden board

red ocher A type of red mineral

sawyer A person who sawed logs

seasoned Describing wood that has been dried for at least one summer

shipwright A person who built large boats

spindle A wooden rod used in furniture making or in constructing staircases

trade A job that requires skill

varnish A smooth hard coating used to finish and protect wood furniture

wainwright A person who built carriages, wagons, and coaches

wheelwright A person who made wheels for wagons, carts, and carriages

woodsman A person who cut down trees

Index

1 2 3 4 5 6 7 8 9 0 Printed in the U.S.A. 1 0 9 8 7 6 5 4 3 2